Life and Laughs
in Limousin

Life and Laughs in Limousin

Merryl Bevan

To order additional copies of this book, contact:
Xlibris Corporation
0-800-644-6988
www.xlibrispublishing.co.uk
Orders@xlibrispublishing.co.uk
301848

FOR TOM
WHO DOES SO MUCH FOR ME

CONTENTS

CHAPTER ONE

THE ARRIVAL

The journey over, coming as it did only three days after our daughter's wedding, was a long, tiring one. The trusty Volvo was laden with seven dogs, loads of dog bedding and various items that hadn't made the removal van. We set off at 6am from our daughter's home and drove to our former home, now bereft of all furniture, to collect the dogs. They had slept overnight (indoors) in the area left from their dismantled kennels. At 7am, fully loaded, we began the drive to the Euro Tunnel. The dogs, being seasoned travellers, were without exception, settled and quiet.

We arrived at the tunnel with time to spare and exercised the dogs, fed and watered them. Because we were arriving with seven dogs and no-one knew for sure if the 4 dog rule applied to each person or to each family we were advised to apply for an import licence from the French Ministry of Agriculture.

I was nervous about the paperwork, which had taken six months, two letters, three faxes and several telephone calls to the French Ministry of Agriculture before it finally arrived. On top of this of course was the usual micro chipping and rabies vaccination. We also had blood tests on the youngest three dogs in case we should need to return within their lifetime, which was not our intention.

The journey on the train was quickly done, although we were the cause of much amusement, carrying, as we did, six English Setters and one diminutive Jack Russell.

I had all the dog paperwork in a folder, their pet passports stating they were in good health and had been micro chipped and had rabies jabs. The precious Import Licence was also in the folder and I prayed we would not meet any hiccups on arrival as we could not, once on French soil, return with four of the dogs who had not had blood tests.

The train ground to a halt and we followed the car in front. Off the train, up the slip road and straight onto the highway!!

NO CUSTOMS. I admit to feeling both relief and a bit disgruntled to find that all the hard work in procuring the Import Licence was not needed. Of course, Murphy's law would ensure had I not got the licence we would have needed it.

The journey to our new home began.

We were unfortunate enough to arrive at Paris during the rush hour but we eventually won through and finally made it to our new home in Limousin about 10;15pm. (we have since learnt the best way was down the coast and head towards Rouen, Le Mans etc).

It was cold, damp and miserable. The dogs were given time in the newly constructed dog run and we made our way wearily indoors. Tom had spent two weeks here during October, cleaning years of dirt and mildew from every surface. He had left the open log fire fully laid and we only had to light a match.

The dim 60 watt bulb revealed that the care he had taken to leave everywhere tidy had been in vain. The two "English builders" who were supposed to be installing the kitchen for us had taken every scrap of wrapping off the units and thrown them in a huge pile in front of the fire. It was a good job they were nowhere around as I think we would both have throttled them. We overcame this by dumping it all outside the back door. Of course, when they came to install it all they told me they couldn't find certain units and were unsure what was what. I gave a pretty tart answer to this, telling them if they hadn't unwrapped everything in an effort to have looked busy whilst doing nothing, then they would have had the references they sought.

The removal van had already been and unloaded all our furniture and placed the stock of koi carp, golden orfe, shubunkins and goldfish that we had also brought with us into their new home, which was a large family pool bought at our local cash and carry and already erected and filled with water by Tom. We also had medication for the fish.

Although our bed was available we were not in the mood to seek out bedding etc at that time of night and sleep in a cold room, because the central heating had packed up two hours after Tom had turned it on, and had refused to work since. The log fire would provide warmth and cheer so we decided to sleep one each end of the corner unit. We made up dogs beds in the "cellar". This is a very large room, dry and warm in winter with three windows in it. Not at all like the cellar you would find in the UK. The dogs were perplexed at first, not understanding what we wanted but soon enthusiastically poured down the steep cellar steps. TOO ENTHUSIASTICALLY!! It didn't take much of a slip but hey ho, a shoulder muscle was pulled on one of the older dogs. Fortunately I had come well prepared with medication to repair pulled muscles from over exuberance (always needed with English Setters) . Our Welsh vet had kindly let me have a stock of the usual medication required at some time during the year. Tablets for upset tummies, tablets for injured muscles, tubes of ointment for eyes and ears, general cleaners for eyes and ears etc etc. By this time they were showing signs of stress after the very long journey and foray into new quarters and Bach's flower rescue remedy came in very handy and quickly settled them down.

Our medicine chest was well packed with necessities for the dogs even if not for we humans.

The following morning saw us arise rather stiffly but full of enthusiasm to begin the transformation of our beautiful but neglected house into our new home.

The dogs enjoyed their foray down into the paddock and delighted in sniffing here, there and everywhere. Tom and I meanwhile delighted in exploring our new domaine and assessing the challenge that was needed to clear the enormous plots of brambles, some 15 foot high, everywhere.

Well, Rome wasn't built in a day they say. I think it was about this time we fully realised the work needed to return the overgrown, bramble infested paddock scattered everywhere with mountainous molehills and years of uncut clumps of rushes, to a flat even meadow. Well, we had never been happy being idle so we viewed it as a project to enjoy, not fear.

CHAPTER TWO

PATRIQUE

One of the first things needed was to call out a French plumber and see if he could repair the central heating. This would give us hot water as well as warming a house not heated for several years.

Patrique's number was duly rung and so began a friendship.

He spoke no English and as yet our French, especially Tom's, was embryonic. I, at least, had done French in school and had scraped through my exams. The CD's of Michel Thomas triggered memory for me and resurrected long dead schoolgirl French. Tom struggled more because, as he explained, only hearing French didn't give it enough substance and made no connexion with the written word. He couldn't recognise written phrases from the pronounciation. PASK to speak PAR CE QUE written. However Tom persevered and being adept at repairing things was able to keep pace with Patrique's requirements before he had a chance to ask. He would hand Patrique a screwdriver when needed or turn off switches etc.

before Patrique had even indicated his requirements. They soon had a rapport between them that didn't need language.

During this time, if the weather was clement, we worked in the garden, as a means of leaving the paint fumes behind. It was at a time when we were digging up old conifer roots that Tom came across the snake. He's not keen on snakes but I don't mind them. He called to me to come and see and even I was surprised to see a snake with so much attitude. It was only about 6 inches long with a triangular head and a white collar around it's dark grey body. It was reared up in the classic pose of a snake about to strike. Wisely we kept well clear of it and Tom placed it on a spade and took it across the lane away from our property. We do not believe in killing God's creatures unless necessary.

The following day I came across another, larger, only this time dead. As we were interested in knowing about it we popped it in a bucket and intended to ask Jean-Claude (our neighbour) about it. A day or so later Patrique came to carry out work on the boiler so Tom decided to ask him. Carrying the snake down to the cellar he held the head and draped the tail around his little finger. Wiggling the tail it looked as if the snake was alive. "Patrique" he asked "quel sort de serpent?" "aspis" replied Patrique, eyes glued to it. "um, serpent toxique?" asked Tom "ah oui" replied Patrique "serpent morte pour chien" asked Tom in his bad French (death for dogs).

"ah oui" replied Patrique, eyes still riveted on the snake. "um serpent toxique pour moi ?" ah oui—docteur" replied Patrique.

Tom then laid the snake down on the workbench and as quick as lightening Patrique had taken his screwdriver out and pinned the snake down behind the head. Tom began to laugh. Patrique looked perplexed. "Patrique—serpent morte" Tom told him and picked it up by it's tail to demonstrate.

Patrique let fly with a couple of well chosen words, unintelligible to Tom, but he also began to laugh. Thereafter a bond of friendship existed.

CHAPTER THREE

POWER TO THE PEOPLE

There was a lot about our new home that needed attention, including the main fuse box. It was old and needed replacement and so an electrician was recommended to us. Keith lived only a mile or two from our home and had already upgraded our electrical points in the kitchen to accommodate our new appliances. At this point, the French electricity board had been contacted to upgrade us from 6 watts to nine. Electricity in France coming in three grades. 6, 9, and 12 watts. The higher the wattage the higher the cost of the electricity. Most French families were on six but with our new hobs and oven etc we needed 9 watts. Keith and Carl installed our new fuse box but as it was changing over from three phase to single phase it entailed rewiring. Poor Keith and Carl struggled for days to make sense of the wiring done. What began as a blue wire changed midway to green and then to red. There seemed to be no sense to it and each switch became a nightmare to trace. Eventually all bar one switch was connected and so we called it a day. The switch was a duplicate at the other end of a room and so wasn't much of a problem. What did become a major hassle though, was trying to cook on my new cooker. If I used the oven and hob together then tried to put on the kettle the trip switch in the outside fuse box would go and the house would be plunged into darkness. Believe me, cooking Christmas dinner was even more of an art trying to juggle what could safely be turned on without tripping the switch. We struggled with this for months, me blowing my top every time I tried to do a roast dinner and Tom dashing down the garden path to reset the trip switch. Eventually after many months of frustration we mentioned it to friends who had been over here a while, only to be told that in the fuse box outside, although the French side of it had been upgraded we needed to upgrade a fuse our side in order to receive 9 watts.

ALLELUJAH !!!

Such a simple thing and VOILA we had no more problems.

During the dry, cold days we worked at clearing the brambles, wet days were spent painting. The wallpaper, beautiful but dreadful colours, had to be painted over. We had intended to remove it and then to emulsion the walls. To this end we bought a wallpaper steamer, but soon found out that whatever the wallpaper paste was it did it's job only too well. After several very frustrating hours I had removed only a very small area (about 1 square meter) and this had come off in postage stamp sized pieces. Every time you tried to scrape, the scraper stuck into the soft plaster work and left marks everywhere. We gave up and admitted defeat. We would emulsion over it all.

Tom was unsure of the likely result but I decided to do the bed head wall and await results. Now, we had been warned the French paint wasn't very good, an understatement if ever was one. French paint is very, very thin and seems to have no covering power at all. So, we had brought all the paint needed with us. I began on the wall with the chosen colour for that room. One coat, two coats, three coats were needed to cover the dark French wallpaper. I hadn't purchased enough emulsion to do three coats per room. So we decided that it would be two coats of white then the last coat of colour. We had, fortunately, brought a large amount of white paint with us for the ceilings so as they only needed one coat, we had some paint to spare. We also purchased some French white emulsion which was cheap but thin but two coats under the colour did work. Of course, this meant each room had to be painted three times, which extended the decorating time extensively. Of course my carefully chosen colour schemes went awry, when I put the contrast paint on instead of looking pale peach it looked strong tangerine and so more time was spent on painting built in wardrobe doors from one horrendous colour to a more liveable shade. Then I decided I didn't want that colour in that bedroom and so I repainted all the walls again.!!!!

WELL, WELL, WELL.

We have a well in the garden, and it is a working well for the house. Sadly age had taken its toll on the large pump in the "cave" and it had seized solid. Tom asked Patrique to replace it and he said he would try to find a replacement pump. As we already had mains water it was not urgent but I did want to be able to use it for watering the garden in the summer. Weeks went by and eventually Patrique said he had found a suitable pump and he would come over to install it. Well, it was a monster, but fit for the job of raising the water from a deep well. Tom had agreed to connect all the electrics necessary and he also primed the pump. When Patrique came to begin work he turned on the pump to test it and then undid the stopper to fill and prime the pump before Tom could stop him. The water which was under pressure spurted out and soaked Patrique. When Tom had stopped laughing Patrique commented "aujour d'hui deux douches" (today, two showers). Patrique now has two words of English OK and YES.

CHAPTER FOUR

IANTO

By the time March came around the weather was bad. Bitterly cold and with several inches of snow. On the first of March Tom took the dogs down the paddock for their usual 5pm walk whilst I showered to remove all the paint I usually managed to leave on myself. Tom had just got back to within a few yards of the house when Scott, one of the two younger setters attracted his attention to a small creature crawling along the ground. It was squealing and Tom's first reaction was Scott had found a rat. However, when he looked at the little scrap of fur it was plain to see it was a tiny rabbit. He picked it up and came indoors with it. Unceremoniously pulling back the shower curtain he showed me the tiny creature. Needless to say we were captivated. We decided that Scott must have found him in the paddock and picked him up and brought him to the house. Setters, being gundogs, have very soft mouths (that is they are gentle when carrying something) and we have had them do this before. What neither of us could understand was WHY a young (about two weeks) rabbit was above ground in such dreadful weather. That night the temperature dropped to around minus ten. Surely the baby rabbit would have died in such conditions?. Of course we had no idea where Scott had found the baby and therefore the only thing we could do was to try to rear the tiny scrap.

So began a relationship that was to bring us much joy and just a little heartache. The first thing to do was give him a name. Well, it was St David's Day when he was found and therefore a good Welsh name seemed appropriate. We called him IANTO (pronounced Yanto). We placed him in a small cardboard box with some hay, a hot water bottle wrapped in a towel and a small piece of carrot. We left him in a room on his own, dark and quiet. He spent the night warm and safe and was still with us in the morning. Now it was obvious he wasn't eating. He had some tiny teeth but refused all offers of normal food that rabbits, even babies, enjoy. Well, he wouldn't live long unless he ate and drank so I decided to feed him milk and baby cereal.

We duly bought some powdered baby cereal in the village and with the aid of a syringe I started to feed him. It took him a while to learn and he didn't like the hard nozzle of the syringe, but in view of the fact he had teeth, a teat would not have been any use. He nibbled the nozzle each time I tried to feed him. Each mealtime saw more going under his chin than in his mouth and we had to wrap a tea towel around him to avoid getting cereal all over his coat. Because we have reared many litters of puppies I know the importance of regularly weighing them. Twice daily means you spot any signs of dehydration BEFORE it is visible to the naked eye. Well, Ianto was holding his weight but not gaining. This called for drastic action so between the hours of 7am and 12am I fed him every two hours without fail. After three days he had gained an ounce. Not much? Indeed it was, it was 50% of his body weight as he had been a mere two ounces to begin with. Indeed I wondered how so small a scrap of skin and bone could contain life. By the end of this time he was taking the food quite easily, although it only amounted to about 5mils each feed. We also had to bath him now in order to remove all the caked cereal from his chin and coat. The sink was filled to about an inch deep with blood warm water and he was placed in it. We only used water but it moistened the dried cereal and then towelled him dry. After the first night alone Ianto didn't like the confines and isolation of his box and so we brought him into the living room with us and the dogs. We replaced the box with a dog cage, but as he could easily get through the bars it was less for containment and more for a safe space away from the dogs. The dogs loved him and soon he was hopping around between paws and noses, completely at home.

He loved his water bottle and would drape himself over it after a meal and sleep. After about ten days I began to think there was something even more strange about our baby rabbit. His ears were getting much longer and so were his legs. Could it be possible our rabbit was a HARE? Patrique arrived one day at the house and confirmed my suspicions. Our Lapin was indeed a Lievre. Patrique saw the cage and told us not to keep him in it but we explained it was Ianto's bedroom only and indeed the door was always open and he had total freedom of the house. Ianto's story is a book in itself so I will only tell you that he thrived, growing ever stronger and more loveable. He decided that the whole house was his to explore and each mealtime when he was called he would arrive post haste from wherever he was exploring. Not long after we found him we watched the video ICE AGE, and soon we were calling "Where's the baby"? when needing to find him for mealtimes. He was a greedy little man and at this would quickly come running for his feed. He brought a great deal of love and joy into our lives and gave us so much pleasure at a time when our self imposed work was getting to be a chore. Neither of us knew anything about hares and I used the internet to get advice. By the time we knew he was a hare, however, we had done several things wrong. We were told they didn't like noise, but he loved to sit on my lap and watch TV. To keep him away from dogs, understandably for his safety in later life. Well, unfortunately he was already used to ours but we did keep all bar the two old ones away from him from then on. He showed no fear of Lucy or Shelley but to isolate him from them meant him living alone in the study as neither Shelley nor Lucy could live downstairs. Lucy had cancer and was on borrowed time despite an operation.

Shelley's hindquarters were not up to the steep cellar steps so we decided to let things stay as they were.

The months went by and Ianto began living outside in both our and next doors garden. He was an extremely intelligent creature and quickly learnt to come indoors via the patio doors. Once inside with the doors shut he would relax and enjoy his supper. In the beginning he would spend as much as an hour or so with us but as time went on he spent less and less time indoors. Always being apologetic but insistent that he just had to go now. If I was slow in opening the doors he would jump onto the back of the sofa and look through the window as if to check what was happening outside.

His tolerance of dogs worried us but one night he arrived before being called for his supper and he sat in the garden waiting. Both the young dogs were out and were not now used to seeing him. Jessica spotted him but I called to her to stay, which she did. However when Scott spotted him the temptation was too much and he galloped over to see Ianto. He had no malice in mind and Ianto's nerve held out until the last minute but then it broke and he ran off, Scott in hot pursuit. Despite my frantic calls Scott took not the slightest notice and chased Ianto into next door. Here the fence held Scott up but not Ianto. Scott was chastised, not for chasing, but for ignoring me. We worried about Ianto but needn't have done. A couple of hours later, when the coast was clear and we called for him he appeared. The incident did leave him far more cautious about dogs so it really was a blessing in disguise. At least he had not been in any danger from Scott although he was unaware of that. He waited until he was called from then on, knowing the dogs would be away. He was even cautious of Lucy and Shelley when he saw them. However it didn't take him long to regain his confidence as Shelley continued to take little notice of him and Lucy ignored him completely as long as he didn't attempt to get in her basket. Ianto continued to visit us all through the summer but gradually became more independent . At around the end of August he stopped coming for his supper but we could always find him in next door's garden, the house being unoccupied. Then he started to go missing for a day or so and we greeted his return with relief, however his absences got longer, turning from a few days to almost two weeks. He was cutting his ties to us gradually. By November we had become used to his absences and our last sighting of him was on the first of November. We didn't realise at the time this was to be the last time we saw him. We returned to the UK for a week in early November and fully expected to see him when we returned. It was not to be. However we did have some hope that he had only returned to the wild and no longer needed us when friends drove over one evening in February. Their first words to us were "We've just seen Ianto" They were both familiar with "the boy" and told us that they had seen a young hare with very large ears and they were convinced it was him. He had been about to cross the road and had stopped and looked at the car and had not been afraid. He was only some quarter of a mile from our home and we cling to the hope that this indeed was our "baby" and he had completely returned to the wild. We still cling to the hope that we may see him one evening on returning home but as yet there has been no sighting of him. He brought us such joy and laughter and we feel privileged to have known him.

CHAPTER FIVE

FIRE AND WATER

Clearing the garden and paddock of many overgrown conifers and trees produced an enormous amount of wood. Not ones to waste fuel we decided to burn it on the open fire. Normally wood should be seasoned for two years and pine was not recommended as it has a lot of resin in it. However we had an open fire, not a closed wood burner so we decided to substitute it a little at a time amongst the seasoned oak we had purchased. The chimney had been freshly swept when we moved in as a condition of our house insurance and so we supplemented the oak with some of the pine throughout the winter. Towards the end of winter, one day, we were watching TV and I noticed a lot of smoke hanging over the paddock. Tom had stoked the fire up with logs and it was roaring away nicely. ROARING being the word. When we turned down the sound on the TV the roaring we thought had been on the programme continued. It was in our chimney. Tom went outside and quickly confirmed the chimney was on fire. Now we had had a chimney go on fire once before in the UK. I had not been particularly concerned, after all a chimney is meant to cope with a fire isn't it? However, on that occasion the firemen had told me that a chimney on fire could be very dangerous and if not attended to could result in the whole house going up. With this dire warning in mind and having great oak beams supporting the lounge ceiling I decided to ring the fire brigade straight away. The French firemen are called Pompiers and the emergency number was 18. Now the pompiers were in Le Dorat some 15 kilometres away and they didn't know where we were. It took some time and two pompiers before I could explain in my pigeon French exactly how to get to us. Tom however had not been idle during this time and had removed the burning logs and ashes from the grate. At least the logs were not still fuelling the fire. Eventually some 20 minutes later the pompiers turned up in force. There were seven of them and they quickly took charge. Up on the roof went one of them and looked down the chimney. There was much chatting between them all and they decided on a course of action, before we knew it he had a fire hose gushing down the chimney to make sure the fire was completely out. Down the chimney came the water bringing with it a great load of ash and soot. This all collected in the grate which was only a flat area without any sort of hearth. Soon the thick black sludge oozed out of the grate and began to make it's way over the marble floor towards my rug. Fortunately Tom had seen what was happening and had anticipated this and had quickly supplied an armful of old dog towels in order to contain the mess. I was certainly thankful that our French house had marble tiles and not a fitted carpet. Job done and they were finally satisfied that there was no danger any more we asked them if they would like "un cafe ou the" a coffee or tea "NON" came the reply "vine rouge" NO, Red wine.

So red wine it was. Tom opened a bottle and all bar the driver had a glass of wine, he accepted a cup of coffee. So with many "Merci's" and "Au revoirs" the good natured pompiers left.

THAT'S THE SPIRIT

In the third bedroom that needed decoration, on close examination, it was apparent that the carpet was virtually new and did not need replacing. A deep burgundy in colour and still losing "fluff" all it needed was a thorough hoovering and shampooing. This of course threw all my carefully chosen plans for colour into the air but as bedroom three and four both needed decorating, we just changed them around. Indeed bedroom four also needed either a new carpet or tiles because of the attention Ianto had given it in the corners, nibbling at the edges and causing large bare patches.

This was not as bad as it seemed as the carpet was already old and we had decided to replace it anyway.

The formula was the same, two coats of white emulsion and a top coat of colour. all the woodwork was also painted and on finishing I shampooed the carpet.

The bedroom smelled of fresh paint and looked superb. The two single beds were set up and dressed in the new duvet covers and it looked fit for a king.

This bedroom occasionally got a quick dust and a hoover but as it wasn't in use was mostly left with the door shut. One day, on opening the door and going in two things struck me. Firstly, there was a depression on the bed covers as if someone had lain on top of the bed. Secondly, there was a very strong smell of tobacco, exactly like that encountered when visiting my dad at home before he died.

I am convinced dad comes to visit us. The smell is intermittent and because the bedroom has been freshly decorated and the carpet shampooed there could be no residual smell from previous occupation.

I told dad that he is very welcome to stay or visit whenever he wants. Strangely bedroom three is precisely the bedroom he would have chosen had he been living with us as it has direct access to the shower room and toilet. We have had some signs that he visits, leaving lights on in the living room, on several occasions, when I

KNOW I have shut off all the lights. Just recently he turned on the air conditioning in the back bedroom and IT DEFINITELY WASN'T ME as I had no idea how to work it at that point. I think dad was playing games and letting me know he was here.

Aren't I scared? Of course not. My dad loved me and would never have hurt me whilst he was alive so why should I be afraid now.?

CHAPTER SIX

THE FEAST

One day in early June, whilst out in the garden, we were called on by our former French neighbour Annick. She was accompanied by Jaqueline and their purpose was to invite us to a fete they were arranging. This was to be held at the end of June in Jean-Pierre's barn if the weather was bad, by the etang if the weather was clement. In my bad French I asked both ladies if we could bring anything to contribute to the occasion but was assured that they required nothing but ourselves. Our friends Keith & Angie and family were all also invited as they lived in the same hamlet as both ladies. We were sure that this was their way of responding to our Bonfire night affair, in which we invited many of the French neighbours and friends that lived within our two hamlets. It was organised by Keith and his family and was our way of trying to integrate with the local French people. We laid on beer and wine, jacket potatoes, hot dogs and beef burgers and, of course, fireworks.

The day of the fete dawned grey and cloudy which turned to rain and a thunderstorm. This was a double edged sword. I was very glad of the rain for the garden but it would put a damper on the Fete. Fortunately about 11 am the rain stopped and although the sky remained grey and cloudy we had no further rain that day. We arrived around 1pm and were quickly given glasses of a beautiful fruit rum punch. As soon as the level in our glass dropped it was quickly filled again. There were huge salvers of canapes on offer and they were really nice. after chatting for a while we were asked to seat ourselves at long trestle tables that had been set up in Jean Pierre's barn This is a new breezeblock barn with sheeted roof and one half was filled with large tractors and diggers. We sat at the same table as our friends but were cowardly in as much as we did not sit amongst the French people because of the difficulty of the language barrier. However both Jaqueline and Annick the two lady hostess' sat on the end of our table. Firstly we were served with a course of French dishes not dissimilar to potato salad with eggs and mixed veg. There was also an enormous platter of home made pate, garlic sausage and a type of continental sausage. With this came jugs of rose wine. Again, as soon as our glass levels dropped they were quickly recharged.

Baskets of French bread were served with this, a lot of chatting was done and everyone took their time over this course. Eventually we were served with the second course. AND WHAT A COURSE!!

We were given huge platters of lamb chops and cutlets. These had been cooked with coarse salt and rosemary by Jean Claude. The lamb was so succulent and the flavour out of this world. Jaqueline told us they were her lambs, (she farms) there was so much lamb I daren't think of how many they dispatched especially as lamb is quite expensive over here.

Accompanying the lamb were enormous pots of haricots vert (a great favourite of the French although they cook them to death) and haricots blanc (white haricot beans like baked beans) Again we were plied with so much lamb we were stuffed and accompanying the lamb were huge pitchers of red wine. Again some time elapsed, thank goodness, and fromages was brought around. There were many different cheeses and they were accompanied by tossed lettuce. Quite what the dressing is I don't know but it is very tasty. When everyone had partaken of their fill of cheese we were given a wine that tasted of honey and was lovely. Next came dessert!! A "cake" of pistachio ice cream, meringue chocolate ice cream and sponge. Jaqueline had made this herself and it was beautiful. Next, yes, believe it or not there was more, came a huge cherry flan, again home made and scrumptious, the ladies not taking no for an answer. At the same time Jaques came around with his home made Cognac. I managed to decline this but the gentlemen had it. Again glasses being filled to the brim. and we're not talking small glasses here either but plastic tumblers. We were then plied with tea or coffee. Annick had made her home (close by) available for those who needed the toilet but initially at the start of the fete Jaqueline had held up an old chamber pot and regaled everyone in French that if you needed a peepee this was available. When she showed the bottom of the pot there was an eye painted inside it!! This was greeted with uproar by everyone.

Our neighbours, called by us Mr & Mrs "Chou"

(cabbage) because of their wonderful and productive vegetable garden, were there and we learned that they are Guy and Madeleine Artigny. By now it was close to 5pm and England were due to play Ecuador soon in the World Cup. A few of the English had the intention of going to watch the match and returning later, but soon, much to everyone's amusement, a van pulled up by the barn, reversed into the doorway and lo and behold there was a TV in the back!! Unfortunately the small aerial was not powerful enough to get a picture. Not undaunted Jean Claude then brought his enormous camper-van to the scene and supplied us with his TV. This was too small so they transferred the aerial to the larger TV. Up went the vans aerial like some flat periscope and lo and behold we had a picture.

A great roar went up from everyone. Jaques then came around with yet another bottle of spirit called "eau de vie" a homemade brew known as "water of life". Tom said it was well named as it was strong enough to revive a corpse.!! When the match was over

Jaqueline proposed a toast to Beckham for his goal!! it was at this time that someone suggested a game of "Petanq", the most popular game in France. Most of you will have seen them playing it at sometime, it is similar to bowls but played with heavy steel balls. The "jack" is called a cochonet (piglet). It was about this time I left to feed the dogs, Mimms, a friend, coming with me. When we arrived back the men were busy with two matches. There was great light-hearted rivalry and much shouting and laughter going on. Everyone was having a great time and Monsieur Chou was so red with laughter I was afraid he'd have apoplexy. Believe it or not Tom and Keith eventually emerged victorious over the French, not an easy thing as it is their national sport and Tom had never played it before. Trish and I had a go and I found it great fun and something I could do without any problems with "the body" so I guess I might be taking it up soon. By this time it was getting late so while everyone was playing Petanq the ladies had changed the paper tablecloths and out came plate after plate of canapes again. Out came the rum punch and it was back to the fete again. It was a repeat of lunch but augmented by two enormous quiches. My how those ladies worked and how busy they had been with all the cooking and preparation. In all we spent over nine hours at the fete and it has got to be one of the nicest days we have had over here.

CHAPTER SEVEN

THE LODGERS

It appeared one night that we had lodgers. They disturbed me during the night and I spoke to Tom, asking him if he had heard the noise. He said it was only the central heating (the radiators do make a lot of noise sometimes but I am used to the sound they make.) Anyway when it happened again he agreed it was a scratching noise. Thinking it was a mouse in the corner of the room Tom got up to put on the light. Now friends who have visited will be aware that it is PITCH BLACK at night and although Tom had a straight walk from the bed to the door and the light switch I heard him bang into the wardrobe, which was far left. By the time he eventually found the light switch he had made enough noise to scare off a herd of elephants, let alone a mouse.

Needless to say there was no sign of a mouse and the noise had ceased. Tom switched off the light and got back into bed. The noise started up again. This time Tom made it to the light switch without trouble. On went the light, the noise stopped.

Off went the light, the noise started, on went the light, the noise ceased. "They're in the roof and can see the light", says Tom. "How?" I asked. "They can see the light shining where the plaster is broken above the light fitting" The next minute we heard a great scratching and slithering above us. "That's not mice that's owls" we both said in unison. So the owls are in the roof, probably starting to nest and making a great noise with it.

They sometimes wake us up at night with their scratching and slithering, I guess there will be some new arrivals eventually. We don't mind the owls, indeed we feel privileged to know they feel comfortable enough to come and use our loft. Perhaps Ianto told them we're a soft touch.!!

THE POOL

The new swimming pool was due to be started in March but the weather put a stop to that.

A cold, wet and windy spring in France with the locals saying it will be a bad summer, probably because we decided to have a swimming pool built with the compensation money Tom received for his back injury. During this spring we were serenaded, as usual, by the nightingales and the frogs, most of the noise coming from the old swimming pool which houses over thirty emerald green frogs. As spring turns to summer the crickets take over and chirp each night.

British friends who come to stay at this time remark on the constant chirping but after a while we no longer noticed it.

At last work began in digging out the pool area in April. The enormous digger arrived and began excavating the soil, piling it up at one end and adjusting the ground levels as he went. The area the pool was sited had a gentle slope down to the paddock so it had to be built up this end in order to keep the pool level.

April turned to May without much progress being made on the pool, except to say we found a snake had set up residence in the old pool and was sunbathing on the fallen liner. When disturbed however he swam away appearing quite at home in the water.

Reluctantly we left him where he was but placed a long pole into the water to afford a means of escape for him should he need one. I was also worried he'd dispatch all the frogs while he was there but as we had no idea how dangerous he might be discretion played the better part to valour. We did eventually rescue him when earth had been placed in the one end, our friend Mike deciding he was not dangerous and he volunteered to go and catch him. However, the snake was less than impressed and proceeded to defecate all down Mike's jeans!!!

CHAPTER EIGHT

A TAXING SITUATION

Now May is the month when EVERYONE has to file their tax report. Not sooner, nor later but only in May.

Tom and I travelled to Bellac to deliver ours, which was for the previous year, not the current one. This is the way they do things in France.

Having travelled to Bellac we decided to motor on to St Junien to arrange for us to have Broadband for the computer. France telecom only had premises in some towns and the one in Bellac had already disappeared as France Telecom struggled to remain in business. (the one in St Junien eventually was closed also and now you have to travel to Limoges if you wish to see them.)

It was already past twelve and, knowing the French habits we decided to stop for lunch rather than arrive in St Junien to find everywhere closed but too late for lunch.

We came to a hotel called Le Rendezvous de la Chasseurs. On entering we were shown through a dining room full of French workers, through another with hotel guests and into a third that was empty. We were shown to a table by the window and presented with the menu. Tom had noticed that the workers had had large cooked chunks of beef with sauteed potatoes and dips.

The chef's special that day was either Fondue de Boeuf or Cote de boeuf, the latter being thirty eight euros for two. As we really only wanted a light lunch we plumped for Fondue de Boeuf, thinking, correctly, that it was what the workers had.

The waitress brought a funny little metal thing and returned with two glass plates with the potatoes on. She returned once more with a large dish of RAW beef. Apparently you cooked the beef yourself on the little stove provided. Now I confess two things, firstly that I believed the beef would be tough and I had visions of chewing forever secondly that if I go to eat out I like to have my food cooked for me. I get to do enough cooking at home.

We recalled the waitress. Je suis tres desoler (I am very sorry) mais je'n peu pas manger comme ca. (but I cannot eat it like this) and much to her incomprehension we asked if we could have the Cote de Boeuf instead. Bien cuit—well cooked.

It will take about twenty minutes she said. OK, no problem.

Several heads appeared at the doorway to the dining room, no doubt to look at the funny Welsh people who sent the fondue back.

In due course our waitress returned. Firstly she brought a small table and placed it to the side of ours, then she brought the plates of potatoes again, finally returning with a HUGE piece of Rib of Beef, large enough to have been carved for about eight roast dinners. She proceeded to carve this on the small table, first of all cutting the bone off. As she did this I noticed the meat wobbling and she kept looking at the knife as she began cutting the beef vertically into two.

Then she dumped each enormous portion on our plates. Upon inspection the top quarter inch of the beef was cooked, the rest was completely RAW.

Here we go again, Je regret (I'm sorry) mais etc In my poor French I struggled on, asking her if the chef could perhaps slice it and then cook it, so, off went the beef and here came the onlookers, popping their heads in to see these crazy people who kept sending food away. In due course the beef came back well cooked and delicious but no, Tom and I won't be lunching there again. They'd probably lynch us if we did!!!!

Mind you we had a good laugh about it at the time.

HOT WATER

Eventually the workmen arrived to construct the pool itself, working to extensive and accurate measurements. Once the shell of the pool had been erected the digger returned to landscape the excess soil. The plan was to remove a good deal of it, as arranged, to dump in one end of the derelict pool and afford a means of escape for any wildlife in it.

We greeted the digger driver one morning and then left to go shopping. On our return we were horrified to discover that the digger driver, taking the easiest course, had simply spread the excess soil right around the pool and almost up to the house. The level of the Cave (cellar) windows were now well below soil level and the winter rains would probably cause it to flood.

We remonstrated with him, he shrugged and refused to understand us. In haste we contacted Francois (the English speaking representative) to speak to him.

Fortunately Francois was easily reached but our digger driver was less then happy about having to remove several tons of soil from the area. Without waiting for Tom to explain to him how to reach the old pool via the paddock (Tom had spent days taking down a row of conifers to allow access to the old pool) he charged off down the lane with his digger full of soil. There had been access to the old pool this way many years ago but time and nature had intervened to such a degree that there was now half an acre of brambles and saplings barring the way.

Not to be deterred he drove in through the gate way, demolishing the gate post as he did, only to find his way totally barred. Back he came, still in a temper, and charged down the paddock from the top entrance. As he did, he drove over shrubs I had planted. Eventually all the excess soil was taken to the old pool and he left, steam still coming out of his ears!!!

It took until mid July before the new pool was ready for use but until October before we also had the Solar Panels fitted. Nothing gets done quickly in France, as we have learnt to our cost!!

CHAPTER NINE

MUSIC TO OUR EARS

The weather at last turned as warm and sunny as the previous year. Of course, it was too hot to do little more than snoozes in the afternoon as the pool was still unfinished. On Saturday we went with our friend Frances to L'Isle Jordain for a meal and attended a music festival being held in the village square. The square was very crowded, with bars and tabacs on two sides. Under the awning of the "host" tabac French musicians set up despite lightning and threat of a downpour but it was at least warm. They proceeded to entertain the crowd with comic songs and humour. In the square there were plenty of both French and English people, the French consuming huge portions of "moules et frites" The last act to go on was the one in which friend Stephanie was the lead singer, the band being called The Surrender Monkeys. They were very good and all the Brits joined in and began dancing in the streets, some rather too enthusiastically. When rain threatened to drench the crowd the proprietor of the Tabac began handing out a load of cafe parasols to ward off the impending rain. Surely not something you would see happen in the UK.? Fortunately the rain held off apart from a few spots which were short lived. We eventually made our way home around 1am.

BROCANTES AND VIDE GRENIERS

During the summer we visited many Brocantes (Antique Fairs) and Vide Greniers (Car Boot sales)

I delighted in finding small pieces of Limoges porcelain, usually eggs, and starting a new collection. I also bought several beautiful porcelain plates to add to the collection inherited from my parents. Tom's fetish was to see as many rusty tools as he could. Seriously, Tom enjoyed looking at all the old tools and implements taken to these events. At the Brocantes the tools would be rust free and oiled with an appropriate price but the Vide Greniers had rusty tools in abundance. We enjoyed these Vide Greniers throughout the summer, usually with Frances, our friend. We would have lunch out and enjoy a well earned rest from the self imposed work at home.

CHAPTER TEN

THE BANK MANAGER

French banks are unlike U.K. banks. Here you have to live within your means and a cheque issued without sufficient funds to pay it will bring down the wrath of the bank. Unless there are extenuating circumstances you will find your account summarily closed, and you will be unlikely to be able to open an account elsewhere. Here you are also unable to open a credit card account. The banks and stores only recognise the debit card. Banking fees are also high and the general attitude seems to be that the banks are doing you a favour holding onto your money. Our local bank in Bussiere opens to customers mornings only. Afternoons are reserved for appointments and therefore you shouldn't expect normal banking services of an afternoon. Our bank manager always seemed to be unhelpful and miserable. One morning, having a doctors appointment and therefore needing money to pay the doctor, we called down to the village to use the ATM machine. Unfortunately it was in the process of being renewed and there was a workman there taking out the old machine. Unable to use the cash dispenser Tom went into the bank to draw out some money. He was refused, and told to come back later in the day. In the end we had to borrow some money from our neighbours.

As the summer came to a close, so did the Brocantes and Vide Greniers, we watched as the geese and cranes flew south for the winter and settled down with plenty of oil and wood for heating the house.

Winter is the time we set aside to clear the brambles in the paddock. It is far too hot to do so in the summer especially whilst they are still growing.

There is a technique we use, I anchor the rake into a large patch of brambles and pull taught, Tom then cuts big wedges out of the patch with the brush cutter. The brambles then can be raked, like large balls of tumbleweed, into a heap where we burn them.

GARDENING'S A TWO EDGED SWORD

Gardening over here can be really rewarding as I've never known things grow as well as they do here, (provided you water during the summer) but it can also be frustrating, as plants get eaten both above and below ground. I have had several shrubs fail whilst others in the same area thrive. When I finally pull the plant up it has no root ball, it having been eaten by some sort of insect larvae. Green lawns are not really possible in summer without using a huge amount of water but fortunately the grass seems resilient. Although we are on well water it is insufficient to water the whole garden, lawns included plus household needs so we let the lawns take their chance naturally. They always seem to pick up once we have a good downpour.

We had a farmer friend, Davy, kindly call over, with his tractor. He offered to trash the paddock down for us as the middle, despite our best efforts, had become overgrown with weeds and brambles. We had hoped he would plough it for us but the winter was so wet and he did not have the time. He told us that his wife, Victoria, is pregnant, which was great news but meant extra work for Davy, because Victoria is now unable to look after the sheep (it's very risky for the baby, because they carry a disease with the risk of abortion). Anyway, we were glad he could at least cut it back. Trouble was that instead of turning sharp left and going into the middle of the paddock he drove down through the trees (the best area of our paddock as it is level and just grass). There the ground was too soft and he made great furrows in the ground, even driving over some rhododendrons I had planted and cutting into pieces a long length of hosepipe we kept there to water the shrubs during the summer. We ended up wishing it had been left, as now we had to try to fill in the deep troughs in order to get it back to some sort of level for Tom's mower. The middle of the paddock was also very soft in places so he also got bogged down there but at least we intend to have that bit ploughed anyway. I expect we will have to wait now until the autumn before getting it ploughed and seeded because it will be too hot and dry through the summer.

CHAPTER ELEVEN

SUMMER IS A COMING IN

April dawned gloriously with temperatures of around 25 degrees, unlike our two previous Aprils which had been made bitterly cold by strong north winds. My plants were jumping out of the ground, my runner beans even having a flower on them. Tom was already using the pool although I declined.

Now the hot weather had arrived the lizards were out in force and we had some emerald green speckled ones that were so pretty. They were quite big being about 10-12 inches long (including tail). Scott loved to watch them, especially the little ones which climb the walls of the house.

Over here we also have very large black bees with royal blue wings and the butterflies have been in abundance. Red Admirals, Peacocks and many I don't know the names of, bright acid yellow ones, cream with black lacing and swallowtails, tiny blue ones, white with orange tips, all the ones we used to see as children in

Wales, sadly some very rarely seen these days in the UK. When summer is at it's height and the wild carrot has grown in the paddock we see a myriad of butterflies flitting from plant to plant. Amongst the many wild flowers we see huge green crickets with gossamer wings. These are so ethereal when flying that I am sure they must have been the cause of the belief in fairies.

PUTTING DOWN GRASS ROOTS

We had another "happening" French style. On our way to the main road we pass through a small hamlet called Chez Lathus Haut and as you leave the last house on your right there is a very large field. This has stood empty for over two years since the owner tore the hedgerow out. At the beginning of winter we noticed a small wooden building like a sentry box had been placed at the rear of the field. This mystified us until some months later when we noticed two caravans parked on the edge of the field. There were some signs of measuring going on. Intrigued we assumed that they were probably going to build a house. Then, as we passed each time we found that they appeared to be planting a garden. Some trees and shrubs had been planted and two aluminium greenhouses had been erected (minus glass), joined by a large flat sheet of metal. They continued to plant and started to mow some areas. Are they putting the Cart before the horse and planting the garden even before foundations are laid? It's seemed crazy to us but that's the French for you. It transpired that NO, they weren't going to build a house; it was merely a "homestead" for the two caravans. Eventually there were erected chicken runs and enclosures for a very large mastiff and other pets.

At a later date they added a large wooden building that resembles an upmarket garden chalet but it is being used as living accommodation.

Another quirk, this year, the adjacent field was ploughed, disked and seeded in the spring. Imagine our delight when on passing, this summer, we see a fabulous meadow full of wild flowers which include cornflowers, poppies, marigolds and bountiful cosmos. It is a superb sight.

CHAPTER TWELVE

THE GAMES PEOPLE PLAY

Friday night was the start of the Rounders season so off we traipsed to Asniers (pronounced ANNY AIR) to participate. Me to clap, as I can't run, and Tom to take part, as he can. There were considerable number of children involved and the teams were picked by two 12 year olds. Not knowing Tom, and with his white hair thinking he was old and past it, he was among the Last to be picked although he kept jumping up and down and saying "pick me, pick me". Well, at last the game commenced and Tom was put out on the boundary to catch balls, which of course never ended up closer than fifty yards as nobody could bat!!!

Half time and we all had drinks and snacks, and then Tom's team were put in to bat. When Tom was in the line up a little girl about 8 year old came up to him and said "would you like me to run for you?" Tom declined as gracefully as he could!!!! Come Tom's turn he gave the ball a great whack and made a whole rounder in one run (rounders are also scored by halves due to the diversity in age and ability of the teams). At the end of the match Tom's team had won by 9 rounders to four and Tom was "man of the match" having scored two complete rounders, despite overrunning, hitting the deck, rolling and just touching base before the ball did.

Well, the forecast was good for Saturday so we went to Gencay (Jon say) to a street market and Vide grenier with Fran and her daughter Lauren. It was a lovely warm day and we wandered through the streets to the accompaniment of the Accordion Band that was playing. I bought another piece of Porcelain for my collection (sorry Cerys) and we stopped for drinks in the square. As lunchtime was approaching fast we decided to return home as Fran had the kittens to feed. We parted for lunch with the agreement that Fran & Lauren would return in the afternoon to swim in the pool while the weather was hot. I confess to taking a much needed nap after lunch but Tom caught some rays and enjoyed basking in the sun until Fran and Lauren splashed him so he decided to join them in the pool.

The telephone rang during the afternoon and Sue invited us all to an impromptu barbeque before going on to the Feu D'Artifice (firework display) at the etang near St Barbant.

We drove to the etang with Sue (leaving anti-social Mike at home) about 10pm. When we arrived it was plain to see that the day had turned up trumps weather wise and all the Brits were cheek by jowl with the hundreds of French already there. All we were waiting for was the skies to darken. As dusk deepened we found a good spot to watch the show and waited. Whilst waiting in the dark I could see something light and almost ghostlike skimming over the water of the etang just in front of me. Birds? large butterflies? too light in colouration for bats surely?. In fact I wasn't sure it was anything other than a trick of the light. Then, across the lake the music started and two rows of lime coloured torches appeared. In this light you could see that it was definitely some half dozen large ethereal bats. Almost as if in time to the music they swooped and glided back and fore across the water in front of us. It was like some wildlife ballet being performed to music. This was short lived though, as the torches died and the fireworks began.

As if in orchestration with the psychedelic music that was being played they shot into the air and exploded with loud bangs, this time accompanied by loud "oohs & aahs" from the crowd. Some of them shot out smaller fireworks that landed on the lake and bounced, bubbled and fizzled before exploding in a hail of multi coloured rainbows. The display lasted for quite some time while the accompanying music added to the surrealistic painting of the skies. Needless to say we arrived home way past midnight, having had a most enjoyable day. However our weekend was not yet over and the following morning, Sunday, we arose early, although not bright, neither of us having had sufficient sleep. We set off in the rain fervently hoping the weather would be kind and we would arrive at the "Grande Brocante" at Verriere and find sunshine. It was and we did. In fact it soon became very hot. We had to "browse" at a faster than normal pace however, as we had to return home in time to attend the local Fete by 12;30. We did find a pretty pair of bedside cabinets for the guest bedroom, a Fisher Price activity centre for Chloe and (sorry again Cerys) another porcelain egg for my collection.

Then it was off back home to see to the dogs before departing to the large barn in Chez Lathus Haut for the fete.

CHAPTER THIRTEEN

FETED AGAIN

This was pretty much the same as the previous year although this year we had contributed to the repast. We had bought a whopping big lump of vintage cheddar cheese, some packets of crackers and I had made a large fruit cake. We were a little bemused to find the crackers being served with the Planters Punch and Canapes but this year we were all far more relaxed with the French in attendance. After the main course was served the cheese came out and the cheddar cheese was a huge hit amongst the French.

After eating myself full, and bemoaning the fact I had no more room for more of the delicious deserts I left Tom playing boules and went home to feed the dogs. When I returned to the fete I brought with me two large photos of Chloe to show our friends who were there. As I began to drive back the heavens opened and we had a deluge. Although the rain had eased considerably by the time I arrived, it was still raining enough to spoil photos, so I tucked them under my top and held them there (just above the waistband of my skirt) so they did not fall out.

As I say, we were all more relaxed with each other this time and the wine and spirits had been flowing freely. Many of the company were "well oiled" including our neighbour Guy (pronounced gee, you will remember we call him monsieur chou, mr cabbage) as I hurried into the shelter of the barn Guy was there and saw me clutching my stomach. He came across and put his hand over mine making a joke about my having an "enfant" in my tummy. To which everyone laughed, including me, but I topped his joke by saying "OUI, j'ai un enfant, une petite enfant" (yes I have a child, a grandchild) and then produced the two pictures of Chloe. Everyone roared with laughter, including Guy. Then the French decided to play Belotte (a card game) and Guy wanted me to play with them.

I declined, not knowing the game, but offered to watch him play to which I gathered by his French and actions that I would be his good luck charm. The game was fast and furious and something like whist but the rules appeared to change as they went along, although there was much laughter and arguing going on. In fact, I suspect it was as well that I couldn't understand them.

Once the rain had stopped the boules players returned outside and I then partnered Tom for my first game since last year. We challenged Chris (next door) and Carl and were 12/10 down with only one point needed for victory by Carl & Chris. You win when you have scored 13 points. Low and behold I pulled an iron out of the fire and Tom and I won 3 points and the game. We fought a valiant battle against Keith and George (despite their heckling "nice arse" comments, mine, not Tom's—there is a benefit from losing over 3 stone) and lost 13/10. I strongly suspect that there are some very sore heads this morning, both French and Brits. Tom was wiser this year and declined the Eau de Vie and homemade brandy sticking to just a few glasses of red wine. Last year he felt decidedly seedy the following day.

It was nice to have this weekend, it reminded us of why we like France so much as we had all been down in the dumps over the rotten weather. You almost EXPECT IT in the UK but not over here. It was probably our fault though. Last year we had the swimming pool built, Tom put in Air Conditioning during the winter and to cap it all I went and bought two summer dresses, my first for about ten years!!!!!

CHAPTER FOURTEEN

PLAYING AWAY

TOURING TURIN

Tom & I left on the 3rd September aiming to be in Turin for the eve of our Wedding Anniversary (36 years, incredible isn't it? I reckon we both deserved medals) Now Turin is a nightmare to drive through but if you're looking for a specific hotel (we'd booked on the internet) then trying to find it is even worse. You could say the strain certainly made 37 years an increasingly unlikely scenario. However, we finally found the hotel, The Jolly Ambasciatori eventually, but not before driving through a rather risque part of Turin where the "ladies of the night" were in full view with thigh length boots, micro skirts and plunging necklines. At least Tom enjoyed this part of the view!!!!

Instead of staying the following day we decided to motor on down to the Italian coast. We stopped in Savona, where I had a very large dish of strawberries and superb Italian ice cream and cream.

Fortunately Tom was willing to share with me or I probably would have been sick.

We drove all along the coast and stopped for the night in a very pretty place called Arenzano. Our hotel window faced the sea and looked over the very pretty coastline. In the hotel I found a leaflet for the Aquarium at Genova (Genoa) so we decided to stop there and visit it. Being newcomers to the city we were amazed at the HUGE amount of scooters the Italians have. For every car there must have been twenty scooters. Italy must be the scooter country of the world, like bikes in China. What was even more amazing were the riders of the scooters. As many young, very slim girls as men and boys and none of them wearing any sort of protective clothing other than a helmet. They drove around in T shirts, shorts and mini skirts with only sandals or flip flops on their feet. They zigzagged in and out of the traffic and whenever you pulled up at lights you were suddenly surrounded by about twenty scooters, all pulling in front of you as the lights changed to green. The amount of cars with dents and scrapes was phenomenal, testament to the frenetic scooters.

The signs for the Aquarium took us down a back street, onto a large part of the port and into a small secure parking area. We were told to follow the blue footsteps to the aquarium. This took us through areas that were being rebuilt and we eventually emerged onto a dock where a sign told us that it was 700 metres away. Some enterprising chap had set up a small electric cart and carriages to take you there. Mindful of my dodgy back and feet we decided to let the train take the strain for the princely sum of 1 euro each. We thoroughly enjoyed the aquarium where we saw sharks, rays, sun fish, swordfish, dolphins etc etc. When we came out we saw a statue that we hadn't noticed before, of a man in old fashioned sea captain's hat and clothes with a telescope. I was just wondering who it could be of when suddenly it moved!! It was someone dressed up with his clothes and face stone coloured and it was very realistic. They also did this in Florence we later discovered and they were very good as well. Also in the dock close by was a huge old fashioned caravelle with a carved figurehead and three masts. It looked to be the genuine thing about 300 years old. One thing we also saw, that there was parking just a hundred metres away from the aquarium. Naturally, when we returned to the car we were hit with a parking fee of 8 euros. Come to Genova and get conned!!!!

MEDITERRANEAN SIGHTS

We then drove further around the coast, driving up and through the mountains where necessary and found a beautiful little town called Santa Margherite on the Italian Riviera. I have seldom seen such a beautiful place and we were lucky enough to get a hotel with superb views over both headlands and the sea. We stopped here for two nights and so enjoyed some wonderful Italian meals. I plumped for sea bass one night and swordfish the next. Tom, never a great fish lover, had bolognaise and steak. On exploring the shops etc we decided to go into the large church. What a revelation!!! It was so very beautiful inside, the ceilings being decorated with exquisite pictures and so much gold leaf it must have cost a fortune. I have never seen anything as beautiful, but it left us wondering if it was to the Glory of God, or to the Glory of Man? Whilst in the church I lit a candle for a relative suffering from cancer, and one for little Madeleine as well.

FABULOUS FLORENCE

From Santa Margherite we drove on to Florence, a city I have always wanted to visit. We again had rather a frenetic time driving around a city we did not know nor had any idea where the "old part" was. We stopped at a couple of hotels where, fortunately, they were full. I say fortunately because it later proved they were in the wrong part of town. Eventually we found the river Arno and a lovely hotel facing it. This worked out just right as all the finest buildings and museums were within walking distance from the hotel. The first night foray (for a meal, no hotel restaurant) found us in a Piazza absolutely astonished at a stunning church. It was so beautiful and was almost luminous in colour, the front being made of very light stone and marble, full of colonnades etc.

The next day as we explored further I was delighted to find so many gorgeous little shops, leather goods, beautiful clothes, jewellery. Indeed, I actually bought several Christmas presents and had decided on a shop till you drop day. In a small jewellery shop as I gazed into the display cabinets I came across a fabulous opal bracelet. Now, opals are my thing and I adore them, but they are costly. The bracelet was stainless steel with gold stops and ten gorgeous large opals. Although light (whiteish) they were full of colour, blue/green and rose pink and sparkled in the light. Knowing how much opals cost I guessed the price would be above me but I figured I might as well ask or I would never know. Now, having had a birthday recently and knowing we were going to Italy I had told Tom I would rather choose a present if I saw something I liked. On asking the assistant the price I thought she had got it wrong and couldn't believe my ears but I kept a fairly straight face and told Tom I had found my birthday present. He enquired the price and got the same figure as me. So, he paid for it by card (and I've checked the receipt) and I became the very proud owner of a fabulous opal bracelet for the very small sum of £130. On reading the guarantee I find it is by an Italian company called Nomination, who specialise in this sort of thing. I looked them up on the internet and they are very fashionable. Needless to say I was delighted.

OH DEAR

My shopping euphoria was to be short lived, however. We stopped for lunch then returned to the hotel to leave our shopping, freshen up and foray forth again. My large handbag had become bogged down with too much bulk so I had bought a small shoulder bag with zips. I transferred essentials like purse and glasses and left the bulk of the "hand luggage" in the room. Hearing all the horror stories of bag snatchers etc I kept my hand firmly holding the strap and the bag zipped up at all times. We wandered around the piazzas gazing at the huge statues and taking pictures and eventually we walked and found the Duomo and were enthralled by it's beauty and size.

We also saw a superb large door with ten biblical scenes sculptured in gold.

We decided to see the inside of the Duomo to see if it was as beautiful inside as out. (It wasn't)

When the queues diminished we stood in line waiting to go in. Someone pushed into the queue by me and said he wanted "information". Unknown to me at the time, although Tom did clamp his hand on his pocket with his wallet in, he cleverly unzipped my bag and stole my purse. I found out my loss when inside the

Duomo and believe me I was devastated. There was more than 450 euros in my purse, not to mention all my credit cards. It may sound stupid but I felt as if I had been violated. We rushed back to the hotel and I phoned Cerys (thanks babes) as I had no information for the cards on me but one of my cards has her billing address so she has paperwork there. She phoned them up and cancelled the cards and gave me a number to phone and cancel my bank cards. We then had a taxi to take us to the Carabinerie to report the theft. Bang went my shopping spree as Tom only had his French card on him and it wouldn't let us have more than 200 euros a day. We had already reserved tickets for the Ufizzi Museum the following day but we decided to leave Florence on the day after as it had completely spoiled this beautiful city for us. We did enjoy our visit to the museum and saw many masterpieces by Leonardo Da Vinci, Titian, Canaletto, Raphael etc and numerous statues in marble. Later in the day we walked over the Ponte Vecchio bridge and were amazed to see so much gold jewellery on sale. Each small shop was stuffed with gold and I fell in love with the beautiful necklaces in 3 different types of gold. I did ask the price of a modest (by their standards) necklace and was told 1800 euros so left it where it was!!!

On Monday we left Florence and drove into the heart of Tuscany with beautiful views and hilltop villages. Our plan was to then go back along the coast through Savona (and call in for another ice cream) and so to the French Riviere. Sadly the "gelateria" in Savona was closed so we motored on, stopping for the night in a very nice hotel in a small Italian town

THAT BANK AGAIN!!!

The following morning we drove towards Allassio and spent a night there. When Tom came to pay the bill with his French debit card it was stopped. Fortunately we had just enough cash to pay the bill but it meant we had to drive into France to discover why, when there were ample funds in the account, the card was stopped. We drove into Nice and found a Credit Agricole bank and tried to withdraw funds, producing the passports as proof of identity. They wouldn't give us money, explaining that there was a 400 euro limit per week on the account. It was only then that we remembered on first setting up the account the bank wanted to know how much cash we were likely to withdraw in a week and set the limit at 400. This was, of course, 3 years ago and we had entirely forgotten it and certainly never expected it to be so rigid we could only take the limit off by calling at our own bank IN PERSON . The Nice bank did allow Tom to withdraw 400 euros but this was for the whole week and would scarcely cover 3 more nights !!!!. So, our beautiful holiday was cut short there and then!!!. Since coming home (boy am I glad to be back in my own very comfortable bed) we have been to a Vide Grenier so I have spent a little more but I bemoan the fact I had to come home without a beautiful Italian handbag, alabaster statue, superb Murano glass etc etc.

One thing that was "strange" was that on three separate occasions I almost turned around to the back of the car to ask Dad if he was OK and enjoying himself. It was a VERY strong feeling and I think Dad did join us on those days as we had some lovely family holidays in Italy when I was young.

Although, on our way home, we drove through parts of France we had never seen before both Tom and I agreed that we had seen nowhere either in Italy or France that we would rather live than where we are now.

CHAPTER FIFTEEN

THE CHRISTMAS MARKET

We have visited the the French Christmas markets before and what a great time we had, seeing people on stilts dressed up as lords and ladies, seen tigers in their cages waiting for a circus display and watched as horse drawn carriages drove around the town. Well, one Sunday in mid December there was a large "Marches de Noel" advertised in my book of Haute Vienne events. It promised many produce stalls, arts and craft stalls, music, spectacles, etc and for the children face painting, pony rides and Father Christmas at around 5pm. It was to be held in a town just outside Poitiers called Jaunay Clan. We made arrangements with our friend Frances and we all set off on a bright and sunny but cold day around 9;30am. It takes about an hour to get to Poitiers so we arrived at Jaunay Clan around 10;30. Heading for Centre Ville we drove around the many streets and into the square. NO MARKET. Driving further around we returned to the main road and tried the other side. Still no market and no signs guiding us at all either.

After searching for about a quarter of an hour we gave it best and decided to visit Poitiers town centre where we would all have a coffee or Chocolat Chaud (hot chocolate) Driving past the airport we stopped at some traffic lights.

WHERE WE STOPPED.

The car refused to go further. Despite repeated attempts by Tom she would only turn over and then would stop. Tom managed to park on the grass verge just after the lights and put out the little orange triangle required under French law. We also left the hazard lights on. To see all the French people gawping at us as they drove past you'd have thought it was an alien spacecraft not a car. Mind you, it WAS a VOLVO perhaps that was strange enough. Tom eventually got hold of the breakdown recovery people and praise be they spoke English. Trying to explain the situation in French may have proved difficult "Mon Volvo ne marche pas" sprang to mind (my Volvo won't work, or literally my Volvo won't march as work in French is travaille, yes it confuses us also.) We were promised that someone would be with us within 45 minutes so to while away the time we played I SPY.

The recovery vehicle arrived to the minute and, after listening to the car start and die, decided it was a garage job. He would tow us to the Volvo garage, which, as luck would have it, was less than a mile away. He would also call us a taxi which they would pay for (covered by insurance). So just over an hour after we had broken down we were on our way back home in a French taxi.

Fran and I sat in the back and Tom next to the driver. There were two reasons I was glad of that. The first being when the driver was speaking to "mission control" as his breath was enough to knock down a full grown camel. The second was his driving. He liked to sit literally in the middle of the road, only swerving to the right when lorries came along. Add to that the pathological hatred the French have of having any vehicle in front of them and their determination to pass it at all costs, and until they can, driving within three feet of the vehicle in front and you will understand why I was glad I couldn't see the road all that well. The miles sped by and so did the charge counter. I'm glad we weren't paying as it came to 158 euros for our trip home. As for the market, well, the book had got it wrong at least twice before so I guess it was wrong a third time. We were rather disappointed as we had been looking forward to all the sights, sounds and smell of the market. Hopefully we will catch another one later.

GOING THROUGH THE MOTIONS

It seems the gremlins were dead set against us just prior to Christmas. In addition to the car breaking down and the missed market we also had a problem with the loos.

We had been having problems when we flushed one loo the other had an eruption of water as air seemed to be forced back up the pipes. The blue bathroom was the main problem, not flushing properly either, whilst the shower room seemed OK. Tom spent days under the house pushing pipes into the system to clear any blockages and also to install an air vent. The problem was there was water in the pipes where there should have been none. Tom wanted to dig up the fosse to check things out but as Cerys and Keith were due to come to us a week or so before Christmas I asked him to wait until they had been.

Then they had to cancel their early visit, planning to arrive on Boxing day, so, as the one toilet was working alright I persuaded Tom to wait until Christmas was over.

BIG MISTAKE.

I should have let Tom do what he wanted because both toilets ceased to function on Christmas Day. Cerys and Keith and Chloe had surprised us by arriving the evening of the 23rd so, although we had a lovely Christmas it was rather fraught with the problems of the loos. Tom and Keith began to dig up the ground above the fosse the day after Boxing Day. I'll spare you the details but we were able to relieve the pressure and flush properly. The call was put into the VIDANGE man and we waited for him to call. All day Friday we waited, Tom trying to save time when he arrived attempted to lift the heavy concrete lid. OOOPS !!!!! both the lid and the crowbar disappeared into the fetid depths. To make matters worse the vidange man never arrived. When we rang we were told it would now be Monday morning. Monday morning came and went and I rang another Vidange man (who also spoke English well so Tom could quiz him about the problem and type of tank) who promised to get here Wednesday before ten am. I rang to cancel man number one about 1pm just before he rang me to say he was in the area. TYPICAL Let's hope the new man keeps his word!!!

HE DID.

CHAPTER SIXTEEN

ALL OF A FLUTTER

A week or so before Christmas, around 4;30 pm, Tom asked me to listen to a noise coming from somewhere at the bottom end of the paddock. It sounded like running water, gurgling and splashing over stones but with cheeps and chirps added. Mystified we looked to the skies for a flock of birds, you can hear the geese coming on their migratory path long before they arrive and thought this must be another flock of birds. However, no birds appeared. A few days later Tom went down to the old swimming pool at night, with his big torch. What a stir he caused. Several hundred birds erupted from the stand of bamboo in consternation. Tom quickly turned off the torch and they settled back down. It was too dark to see what they were, only their size, which was about blackbird size. The following morning, early, Tom saw them all stream past the bedroom window but again it was not light enough to see exactly what they were. That night about 4;30pm we watched as at least several hundred starlings flew in formation, twisting and turning and adding yet more and more birds, until a huge flock of thousands suddenly descended on the stand of bamboo and dropped from sight.

The noise we had heard was their wings as at least three thousand birds jostled for perches among the bamboo canes. They roost in there each evening, having plenty of cover from the weather. I must confess we feel rather honoured to have them on our land. When living at Avondale I loved to see the starlings waddle their way up and down the lawns but sadly they disappeared and it is years since I've seen very many of them. Now I know where they all went. TO FRANCE!!!!

REMEMBER THE OWLS?

Do you remember the owls in the attic, scratching above the bedroom ceiling? Well, one night Tom went to bed early and was fast asleep when I eventually joined him. About ten minutes after getting into bed I heard a rather loud scratching noise that appeared to be coming from somewhere in the room. Thinking it may be the owls again I took little notice and started to drop off to sleep. Then I heard movement actually in the bedroom.

I jumped out of bed and put the light on, waking Tom in the process. "It's the owls again" said Tom. "No" I said, "this was in the room" But I found no sign of anything and turned the light back off and got into bed again. I was almost asleep when something touched the back of my hand, making me jump and immediately become wide awake. Again I got out of bed, turned on the light, searched and found nothing and got back into bed yet again. Naturally I woke Tom up again, which made me unpopular. Once more, just nodding off to sleep and yes, I heard something moving around in the bedroom. Again we went through the whole procedure, this time Tom getting out of bed, fetching a torch and checking under the bed . NOTHING. "You must have dreamt it" he said. Well, had I?

I suffer from catalepsy (when the body sleeps the brain switches off the motor muscles so you are paralysed, other wise you would sleep walk. With catalepsy you wake up but the brain has forgotten to switch on the movement and although awake you are unable to move, this also causes hallucinations), perhaps this was one?

Eventually we settled down and went to sleep. About 8am, just as it was getting light Tom woke me up saying "There's a mouse on the curtains" and so there was!!

A real cutie with big ears. Seeing us he quickly ascended to the curtain rail. From underneath we could see him running back and forth along the rail.

Tom fetched a broom and tried to knock him onto the floor so we could catch him. He eluded us.

Then Tom went to fetch a box to knock him into so we could put him outside. While waiting for Tom I spoke to the mouse. "We don't want to hurt you at all sweetheart, we just want to catch you to put you outside, but of course you don't know that."

Tom returned with the rigid plastic liner from the pedal bin. "If I can I'll try to knock him into the bin" Just then, believe it or not, the mouse starts to climb DOWN the curtains towards where Tom stood holding the box. Nearer and nearer he came until he was about ten inches from the box and Tom quickly banged the curtain from the other side and he just plopped into the box. You'll never convince me it was coincidence. I reckon that mouse knew exactly what I said to him. Strange HUH?

Tom also believed he dropped in to see us from the gap above the light fitting so that morning he refitted it and closed the gap.

CHAPTER SEVENTEEN

GRAVE(L) MATTERS

Having finally finished the work of edging and planting new beds alongside the swimming pool fence at the rear of the house, and on all the paths surrounding the house, it was time to put the finishing touches. This meant laying a cosmetic covering of gravel everywhere. Our Scottish next door neighbour being a quantity surveyor soon provided us with the figure needed to cover this vast area. 16 cubic metres, which translated to around 23 tonnes. We tried in vain, at the local quarries, to get gravel identical to that already down but as so much time had elapsed from when it was first laid (probably around 1965) this was not possible. So, armed with a jar of the existing small stuff we drove to L'Isle Jourdain where there was a Tout Faire that sold gravel.

Could they help, yes. They showed us an ideal sample of creamy white gravel that we thought would look good.

MALHEUREUSEMENT (unfortunately) they could not supply the gravel in the quantities we required so they gave us directions to Gencay where the company there dealt directly with the quarries that mined it.

Once arrived at Gencay (with friend Fran, as we were all going on to Poitiers for a day out) we duly showed our jam jar to the man at the counter. He directed us to a display and VOILA, there was our creamy gravel. Explaining that we wanted 23 tonnes he drew up a devis (estimate, but binding for 3 months). He explained that we were just outside the free delivery range but if we agreed to take 28 ton (the full load of the camion) then delivery would be free. This we did and the devis was duly produced. 650 euros. I confess I was pleasantly surprised, I though it would be dearer. Now comes the crunch bit. At that time our bank funds were low as we were coming to the end of the year's pension, but not close enough for the next year. So, armed with the devis (a legally binding price on their part) we went happily off to Poitiers. That was in March. By the third week in June funds were in and so we decided to order the gravel. As it happened we had also to go to Poitiers that day so we thought to do it on the way. It is much easier in person than on the phone, especially if you have a devis to show them.

MALHEURESEMENT we failed to find the devis. We both remembered we'd put it somewhere safe, but for the life of us couldn't remember where that somewhere was. AH well, we knew what we wanted so all we had to do was order it again.

The best laid plans . . . . as they say. On arriving at the office we went directly to the gravel and took a sample. This, please, 28 tonnes. he typed in the details on the computer and produced a devis of 1097euros. Oh no, that's not right. Well, that's the cost of what you showed me said the French man. (bearing in mind our conversation is all in French, if a little laboured on my part. However, you can have this other sample for the price of 650 euros. Unsure now of what we'd originally seen, (due to the 3 month delay) and unwilling to pay the price of over a thousand euros Tom, decided to leave it and when we returned home to search for the original devis.

The following day Tom had the brainwave of where it was. Still in the catalogue from Tout Faire. Off we went to order the gravel. Now, the man recognises us and takes the devis from us but proceeds to type out a completely new devis indicating that the original devis is for the cheaper stuff he showed us yesterday. He then destroys our original devis. Neither Tom nor I had thought to check the coding on the original to the coding on what he showed us, trusting him to give us what we'd originally had. BIG MISTAKE Well, it was not as nice as the other, being less uniform in size and colour, but still suitable for our purpose. OK. We order the gravel and await it's arrival. It duly arrives at the promised time, the driver ringing for directions. I was busy in the house cleaning and Tom met the lorry, guiding him in reverse up the drive to the rear of the house. The driver produces the delivery note for signing and asks for the cheque, which Tom duly writes. He then climbs back into his cab, tips the back up, out rushes the stuff in one great whoosh, and off he drives.

Tom then inspects the load. MALHEURESEMENT or rather MERDE. It's not the right stuff.

There sits this malevolent mountain of yellow dust interspersed with great lumps of stone some four or five inches in size. No way can this be spread out and walked upon. They've delivered the sort of stuff you lay on soil to form a firm base before laying gravel.

We both of us feel sick.

This feeling lasts for a week or more while we struggle to write to them in French, complaining that what we ordered (as seen) was not what was delivered. Back comes the reply, the gist of which was that you wouldn't pay the price for the white stuff and ordered this instead but as a gesture of good will I can offer you the right stuff at a reduced price (150 euros reduction). All well and good but what do we do with 28 tons of something we can't use, have no need of and have already paid 650 euros for?

And then we start to remember our original visit. We took the jam jar of existing gravel to show them exactly what we needed. And they gave us the devis which they have now destroyed. Did the original devis have the wrong PRICE against the right gravel?

and did they decide to start afresh because of this. Why could they not stick to the original devis?

Well, to argue the point we needed a fluent French speaker, preferably someone French who could argue the case for us. Fortunately we were very friendly with a lady whose French classes we had both attended. Would Maguy help us?. Maguy would and did. I followed some of the rapid conversation but not enough to understand. Maguy translated and eventually a compromise was reached. We would have the white gravel at the correct price and they would take back the load of unwanted gravel, as long as we would provide the equipment to load it back onto the lorry. So, hopefully, we will be able to bring this to a close.

Eventually, after waiting for everyone to come back from vacation etc we did receive the correct gravel and our farmer friend Davy used his farm machinery to reload the unwanted gravel onto the camion that arrived bearing the correct sort. It was a busy week, that week, where Tom barrowed 100 barrowfuls of gravel per day, whilst I raked it all level. But we got the result we wanted and the house looks beautiful in its setting.

IT'S A WILD LIFE

Since moving here we have been delighted at the abundance of wildlife that is all around us. We have watched while the buzzards fly higher and higher into the sky, riding the thermals and calling to each other with their mewing cry, so like that of a cat. To see them swoop to catch some unseen creature is fascinating, we have even seen one flying across the paddock with a large snake gripped in his talons. The bird life here is varied and different from those seen at home. We have both seen and heard Golden Aureoles flying over the paddock, watched as Pheasants and Quail wander the lanes and viewed Hoopoes search the lawns for large mole crickets. These live in holes in the ground and the Hoopoes beak, being long, thin and curved slightly, is ideal to capture their underground prey. They look like little prehistoric dinosaurs with the long curved beak and the folded crest sticking out at the rear. We also have Black Redstarts, Jays in abundance, Woodpeckers of every colour and Owls by the parliament. There are several species of Owls to be both heard and seen. The Barn Owl is here in abundance, having, as it does, a myriad barns in which to rear the young. We also have Screech Owls, Tawny Owls and Little Owls. During the nights of April and May the Nightingales can be heard singing throughout the dead of night, often accompanied by a chorus of frogs who compete with each other and those in adjacent waters. Whilst working down in the paddock we have come across hedgehogs, snakes and slowworms as well as several species of lizards, great big bugs and beetles, and crickets large and small . At the etang just opposite we have a pair of Coypus living.

The butterflies I've already mentioned but we also have unwelcome insects such as huge ginger hornets which ignore you provided you leave them alone. The hornet's sting is dangerous, especially for children and old folk. Here you buy a vacuum kit to take out the poison, and you will need a visit to the doctor also. We also have the unfriendly frelons.

These are the European hornet, built like an overgrown wasp. Their sting is only as dangerous of that of a wasp but due to the chemical make up it is ten times more painful than a wasp sting, as Tom found to his cost one night when going to close the window. He did not see the frelon on the handle and it stung him at the base of his finger. It was in a position that we were unable to use the kit and the following day Tom's hand and arm had swelled up and were obviously infected, which necessitated a visit to the doctor for antibiotics.

We've found salamanders in the old pool, and newts by the new pond. We've seen deer in the fields and hares on the highways, toads in the swimming pool, bats in the cellar and newts in the rockery. We've found rare salamanders, so very beautiful in their black and yellow suits and we also have wonderful large luminous green lizards, the males having turquoise blue heads.

As yet we've never seen a sangleur (wild boar) but as these are unpredictable creatures and noted for their bad temper we don't feel we have missed out too much.

We are also privileged to be directly under a migratory path for the geese and cranes that fly both north and south for either summer or winter. It is an amazing sight to see skein after skein of birds flying in formation and calling to each other the whole time.

Indeed they are usually heard long before they are seen so we have time to look up as they pass. They often start to circle in the sky above the house, riding the thermals to gain extra height and waiting for the laggards to catch up with the main flock.

This year, at the nest building stage of the birds, we noticed a little Wren trying to build a nest. Where? Under the tarpaulin that covered our patio furniture on the terrace. I watched as he (yes, it's apparently the males that build the nest) brought beak full after beak full of moss, landed on the floor and then flew up under the table. Oh dear, much as we hated to stop him, if they raised a brood there then our patio furniture would be off limits most of the summer. Reluctantly Tom undid the tarp, and removed the moss, leaving it handy on a nearby wall. However, he was a persistent little devil and he next tried to build a nest in the patio umbrella. Yet again we needed to deter him, and we removed the moss from the top of the collapsed parasol.

He finally got the message and went elsewhere to build his nests. (Apparently the male builds two or three and the female chooses which she wants).

Then, one day in late July I was sat at the bench and table which are alongside the abris (a bit like a car port) of the garage. This end of the garage houses insulated kennels for the setters. I have two cone shaped hanging baskets of geraniums hanging from the abris. I watch as a Jenny Wren flew from the hedge into one of the baskets. Back she came, into the hedge and within a few minutes flew back to the hanging basket again. Curious as to what she was up to I investigated the hanging basket, only to find a perfect little round nest with a small entrance hole skilfully attached to the moss lining the basket.

Almost invisible as it is made of the same moss and disguised by the trailing geraniums. She was quite unconcerned by the proximity of both we humans and the dogs.

During one of her absences Tom put a finger in and could feel a fledgling. We watch, day by day, as she continued to feed the little one. One time Tom saw the baby right at the very edge of the nest entrance. He appeared to be affected by the very hot weather and was getting some fresh air.

One day, sadly, Tom found the sole youngster on the floor of the abris, dead. It appears he may well have fallen from the nest. He was almost fully fledged.

Being August it is unlikely she will have another clutch of eggs but we won't disturb the nest until late October when I take all my geraniums into the greenhouse.

Last year, at the close of the summer, due to inclement weather, the patio umbrella had been closed down for a few days. When the weather brightened I sat at the table and noticed what looked like mouse droppings at the base of the umbrella. With great curiosity I slowly opened the umbrella to find two tiny bats had installed themselves at the top. We closed it back up until it was dusk and then opened it again when they promptly took flight. Tom then dismantled the umbrella so the bats would find themselves a more permanent place to live out the winter.

FRENCH CONNECTIONS

Just before Christmas we found that we kept losing connection to the Internet. Tom thought it might be the modem and purchased a new one in Poitiers. No, that didn't fix it. Time for an engineer.

Well, as neither of us is fluent in French it caused a few problems. Telephoning to France Telecom we kept getting automated response. ie For bill queries press one, for accounts press two, etc etc. Trouble was understanding it all, as the voice spoke at a speed we couldn't keep up with and while we were still deciphering the first sentence she was on sentence three. However Tom persisted and eventually managed to get an actual person to talk to. He booked a "rendezvous" for an engineer to come. He arrived Christmas Eve. We were well impressed, sadly though he was unable to find the problem, saying "c'est bizarre" as he tested each phone socket. Eventually he left, promising to book another call for the line engineer, as he thought it was a fault on the line into the house, which was not his territory.

We wondered if we would eventually see someone at all or whether we would have to go through the whole frustrating performance again.

Well, YIPPEE on Boxing day (which is NOT a French Bank holiday) an engineer arrived.

This time, despite Tom telling him he thought it was a problem with the line coming in, he tested everything his colleague had done, again. Once more "Trez Bizarre" He then decided to check out the telephone exchange in Bussiere. Back he came, that was OK. Try again, NO, still no Broadband connexion. He steadfastly refused to climb the ladder he had to check out the incoming line. Off he went again to Bussiere, back he came. NO, he'd had enough (he was full of a cold) and he left, telling us he'd put in a call for the line engineer. OH GREAT, here we go again!!! AMAZINGLY, on Saturday, New Year's Eve three of them turned up in two vehicles, one with a Cherry picker attached. They checked the line, yes

Broadband coming into it, our end in the house, no Broadband. Out came the boss with his IT machine. "Ahh, no broadband, we are too far from the exchange you must be within 16 kilometres. Tom told him we are within 3 kilometres of the exchange. "Oh, well", he turned on the machine. "Ah, it's not working" "Yes it is" says Tom, "Oh, oui oui, so it is". "Only .5 strength though", "No" says Tom, it's climbing to 2.0 and we have 2.4 normally" "Ah oui, oui". EVENTUALLY they repair the line outside coming in to the house. That's the French for you, they desperately try to find reasons why they cannot do the job instead of getting right down to it in the first place. They got their own back though as they turned the speed down from 2.4 to 1.2

THINGS THAT GO BUMP IN THE NIGHT

Remember the visits from my dad? well, one night when I was soundly asleep we had a "Happening". It was fortunate that Tom had just woken from sleep because there was an almighty BANG and I nearly levitated to the ceiling with fright. Tom quickly reassured me, saying he thought his dressing gown had fallen to the floor but on turning on the lights it was plain to see a picture had fallen from the wall.

On inspecting this in the morning and on examining the twine it appeared to have been cut through as it was a clear precise cut with no sign of fraying. Friends say it must have been dad again but I don't think he would have frightened me like that.

This also happened once more when we were away and Fran was dog sitting.

GOT THE WIND UP

This winter we've had various sorts of weather, similar at times to the UK. We had the freezing temperatures and some snow, but although colder than the UK we did not have anywhere near the amount of snowfall. We also experienced some storms. The house often gets high winds blowing around it and one evening whilst watching TV we heard the wind pick up until it was shrieking around the house like an express train roaring past. Never, in all our time here, had we heard winds like it. I thought of all the trees in the paddock and thought it most likely we would lose one or two of the pine trees, one tree that did concern me was a large dead oak not far from the house. This was only a trunk with four bare limbs, having lost all other branches and all its bark over the years. I hoped that as it had virtually no "head" to catch the wind it would not come down. We went to bed around 11pm but the wind was so ferocious and noisy it made sleep impossible, even after shutting the bedroom shutters tightly. We both got up for a cup of hot chocolate and Tom went into the study to look out the window which overlooks the pool and greenhouse. Mystified he saw some sort of sheet flapping around the rear of the greenhouse. Unable to decide what it was he donned shoes and dressing gown, grabbed a torch and investigated. I watched from the patio terrace as the torchlight lit up the scene. OH DEAR !!!! the large dead oak tree had succumbed to the monstrous winds and had fallen straight across the back of my poor greenhouse. The flapping we could see was the fleece I had laid over my more tender plants to stave off the frost. My poor greenhouse was creamed. Broken glass lay everywhere and two of the four limbs of the oak were entangled among the twisted pieces of aluminium and glass that had been the rear portion of the greenhouse.

By the stark light of day the damage was almost total.

Two thirds of the whole greenhouse had been smashed and several sections of aluminium were twisted beyond all repair. It was an insurance claim job!!!! Tom took photos of the oak in situ amongst my plants and pots and of the damage done. Down he went to the Insurance office. Ah !!! the tree was dead and therefore should have been taken down, but there was some doubt as to who owned the tree. It was in the middle of the hedgerow but did it belong to us or to Madame Giraud? We were told to check the "Cadastre" at the Mairie. This we did, but there was no indication as to ownership. All we knew was that the fence-line was her responsibility and that she had cut down numerous branches from trees along the line and never stated they were ours. Back to the insurance office. "AH" you have to ask the Mayor, he will know" "why?" thought we as it is a new Mayor who has only been in office several months and who is also the village doctor so he has little time to spare. "No no, he has jurisdiction over these matters". Off we trot back to the Mairie once more to make a "rendezvous". Of course, the lady in the office recognises us and asks why we want the appointment. We explain. Then comes a gentleman who is the Mayors "adjutant". We explain the dilemma, whose tree is it?. "If it is on your side then it is your tree, but if she has cut trees down on the fence line she cannot do that unless they are her trees" "She is responsible for the fence" say we, "then it is her tree" says the AJ "but she has put the fence behind the tree" we say "then it is your tree" says he. Round and round we go and end up nowhere. The consensus of opinion being it could be her tree or it could be ours. Back we go to the insurance office again and explain what has been said. ie nobody knows whose tree it is and the insurance won't act until we can determine the fact. We have arrived at an impasse. It looks as if we're stumped. Disconsolately we return home.

The following day a message has been left on our answer phone, it is the insurance office asking us to go down as they may be able to resolve matters. Tom goes on his own as I am busy cooking. He comes back and is delighted to tell me that after explaining our difficulty to the Insurers (we are good customers as all our insurance is from them) they will cover the cost of a replacement with a limit of 2000 euros. This is good news indeed as this will more than cover the cost of a replacement . . . . and finally my new green house arrived and Tom erected it for me on the base of the old one. We were also able to salvage some of the old one and in due course Tom erected it at about 2/3rds the size it used to be.

CHAPTER EIGHTEEN

TEMPUS FUGIT

In due course the year progressed and my birthday came around. Our good friend Mike also has a birthday in August, and like me he was turning sixty. Mike always has a BBQ for his birthday, attended by numerous family and friends. This year we agreed to host a joint BBQ, at Mike's house as usual. The band was booked, the guests invited and Cerys pressed to attend with the children.

Come the day large trays of chicken legs, sausages, kebabs, beef burgers and numerous salad dishes wended their way into Sue's kitchen, ready for the party. Chairs and tables were commandeered from friends and neighbours and the abris was set up for the band to use.

The evening went very well, Cerys, Tom and the grandchildren duly had a dip in the pool, long before other revellers took the plunge. After changing and having something to eat they were driven home by Tom around 7pm as it was past the children's bedtime. As the evening progressed much merriment was made and the pool soon filled with people swimming. The French people also took the plunge despite the absence of swimming costumes. One French gent was thrown fully clothed in the pool and he swam around gradually divesting himself of his garments, stopping only when he got down to his underpants. When he finally left for home he took off on his motorbike, waving farewell to us all and clad in only his wet underpants.

A DAY AT THE RACES

The racecourse just outside Le Dorat hosts three meetings per year. We usually attend at least one of these meetings every year and have a fun day out. The first meeting was on June thirteenth and this year we arranged to go with friends Jane & Mike, planning on a picnic in the grounds, where picnic benches are provided. Although the weather had been wet all week the forecast was for sunshine and showers on Sunday. Thankfully although the skies were relatively cloudy and occasionally threatened rain we had no showers. The first two races Mike backed the winners and Tom had a placed horse. Mike's luck continued, either backing the winner or a placed horse. Jane also backed a couple of placed horses, as did Tom.

ME? No, nothing!!! never have I gone racing without backing at least one winner but the first five races eluded me. All to play for on the 6th and final race. Should I back number 1 or number 6? I settled for number 1. Off they went and my superb looking horse was lying easily in third place. Around the course they went and number 1 swept on majestically. he was going so easily, well within himself even though the others were straining. On they came, over the hedge off to the right on and around the course. Oh what an easy winner I was going to have!!!! The following pack of 8 or 9 pulled up . . . . what was going on? By this time the three leaders were galloping up the hill, furlongs in front of the others. Those that had pulled up retreated back down the course to the big hedge again, then the 3 on the hill pulled up. OH DEAR they had taken the wrong course. Those that had initially pulled up had realised this and thus returned to take the right course. And the winner?

Number 6 of course!!!!!!

AND JANE HAD BACKED IT!!!!

It was certainly unlucky thirteen for me that day.

WET AND WILD

Last week, Tom found a tiny bat clinging to the skimmer at the end of the swimming pool. When Tom picked him up he was cold and wet. Had he tried to catch an insect in the night and got too close to the water? We brought him indoors and Tom got the hairdryer. To start with the bat bared minute sharp teeth at us but so small was he, he could not have bitten even the smallest finger. I held him while Tom used the hairdryer and he soon dried off and began to warm up. He quickly realised we were trying to help him not hurt and soon he was warm enough to move around and he began climbing up my arm.

Tom took him to the garage where he promptly hung upside down on a beam and seemed to settle. Several hours later he had flown away.

I looked him up on the internet and he was a Pipistrelle . I had not realised they were so very tiny, smaller even than a mouse.

Next on the agenda is something entirely new and amazing. Tom and I were walking in the swimming pool enclosure discussing where to plant a grape vine. As we got to one corner by the hedge Tom spotted a fawn. No bigger than Jessica in height but far far smaller in body and weight. How he had come to be there we've no idea but our presence panicked him and he tried to get through the fence, which was impossible. So spooked was he that he dived right into the hedge but found his way barred by fencing on the other side. He then crashed through the middle of the hedge charging along it looking for a way out. The field fence however carried on all the way down so Tom hopped into the field and turned him back. He then burst out just behind our greenhouses and ran towards the paddock. He totally missed the open gateway and squirmed through the sheep fencing we have along the post and rails. He went pronking down the paddock on all four legs.

We did not pursue him but Tom did walk down the lane and open the bottom gate so he could get out and hopefully return to his mother. Quite where she was we don't know, I'd only wished we'd had the camera.

A MOVING SITUATION

Cerys, our only child, has emigrated to Australia from Wales. Like most mums and dads we miss her and her family a great deal and are now faced with the situation do we join her or do we stay in France? Well, we decided to see OZ before we made any commitment.

We departed from our home in the early hours of November 8th, heading for the UK and Helen's home. Jessica, the last of our setters could not be put into a boarding kennel for a duration of 8 weeks as we did not know how she would react. If she pined and refused food, never having been in a boarding kennel and never left alone for more than a few hours, we dared not risk her starving to death as we could not quickly return home. So, fortunately, Helen offered to have her. Helen has Jessica's brother Max and they were often walked and went to shows together. We knew she would be happy with Max and Helen although we wondered what she would make of Helen's two rescued dogs Leo and Layla.

We needn't have worried however, as they all quickly became friends.

Our minds at rest we set off for Heathrow the following day, staying overnight in a hotel and departing for the airport after leaving the car in the long stay car park.

After checking our baggage in and going through security we made our way to the Duty Free shop. Now Keith (Cerys' husband) had said that single malt whisky was very expensive in Australia so I decided to get him some for Christmas in the Duty Free shop. They had an offer on his favourite Glen Morangie but when we went to purchase it were told that as we were stopping in Brunei we would not be allowed to take it into the country even though our eventual destination was Australia. I was rather miffed but off we went to the Business class lounge for Royal Brunei. Having had breakfast there I decided to ask the woman on the desk if it was right that we could not purchase whisky because of the no alcohol rule of Brunei. She said that if we were only changing planes in Brunei and leaving for Australia then we could have the whisky. Really pleased at being able to buy Keith his favourite tipple off I toddled to Duty Free where I bought two bottles for £50. The journey by plane was very pleasant and uneventful. We stopped at Dubai for an hour or so, leaving our hand luggage on the plane as we weren't changing planes, then off to Brunei.

At Brunei we were changing planes so our hand luggage came with us. Off we went through the doors, around the airport and in through the security section once more. The usual performance, baggage through the x-ray machine, us through the metal detectors. OH DEAR, when they saw my bottles of Whisky she told me I couldn't take them. I was furious. Not only had I checked it would be OK but we were LEAVING BRUNEI for Australia so the alcohol rule did not apply. This I kept repeating, rather like a mantra!!! We each struggled for possession of the bag with the whisky and it was only Tom's intervention that made me reluctantly give up.

He was convinced I would end up in the clink if I persevered. Eventually, after voicing my disgust and complaining to the staff on the Royal Brunei airline I was brought to realise that it was not the fact it was alcohol BUT the fact that it was liquid and AUSTRALIA would not allow it into Brisbane if it was in hand luggage. Supposedly down to terrorists again BUT as we were LANDING in OZ and not proceeding to another aircraft this was a mere ploy.

Amazingly, after disembarking at Brisbane we were channelled through the AUSTRALIAN DUTY FREE. WHAT A CON !!!!!

As they say, the road to Hell is paved with good intentions.

So started our "holiday of a lifetime".

I won't go into detail of our holiday except to say it was wonderful to spend so much time with Cerys and family and we got to know our grandchildren very well. Mind you we soon learned two under five's 24/7 takes some getting used to.

Unfortunately, our arrival started the end of a fourteen year drought and the beginning of torrential rain and floods. Of the six weeks we were there we had rain for almost four weeks.

We did, however, help Cerys to move into her new house on a lake.

Did we like OZ? Yes and no.

The area of the Gold Coast Cerys lives in, adjacent to the coast, is very built up and commercialised. Too much for Tom and me. We hated it. In the hinterland, behind the mountain ranges there was not enough open land and fields as most of the area is covered in forest. What little open land there is, is expensive. On a plus side the houses are very attractive and the areas are well kept and clean. Standards are high and the people very friendly. I thoroughly enjoyed shopping and the steak and bacon were superb, far better than can be got in France. However, Australia is very expensive. Could we afford to live there? Well, for now, we have decided to stay where we are. Once Cerys and family are truly settled and the housing market over here has hopefully picked up we will look again. I've no doubt we will eventually move there as we want to be with our daughter and family and watch the grand children growing up. But for now we'll continue to enjoy life here in France.

Who knows, perhaps the next book will be titled "Gossip and Grumbles on the Gold Coast" or "Quips and Quirks in Queensland!

· ·